This journal belongs to

FIVE THINGS
I'm Grateful For

In a world full of chaos, ground yourself with
the beautiful things in your life.

FIVE THINGS
I'm Grateful For

In a world full of chaos, ground yourself with
the beautiful things in your life.

FIVE THINGS
I'm Grateful For

In a world full of chaos, ground yourself with
the beautiful things in your life.

FIVE THINGS
I'm Grateful For

In a world full of chaos, ground yourself with
the beautiful things in your life.

FIVE THINGS
I'm Grateful For

In a world full of chaos, ground yourself with
the beautiful things in your life.

FIVE THINGS
I'm Grateful For

In a world full of chaos, ground yourself with
the beautiful things in your life.

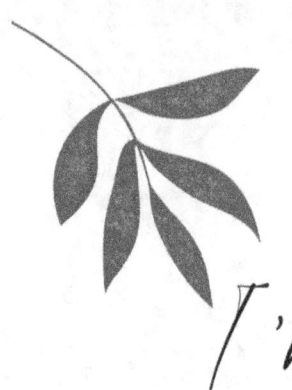

FIVE THINGS
I'm Grateful For

In a world full of chaos, ground yourself with the beautiful things in your life.

FIVE THINGS
I'm Grateful For

In a world full of chaos, ground yourself with the beautiful things in your life.

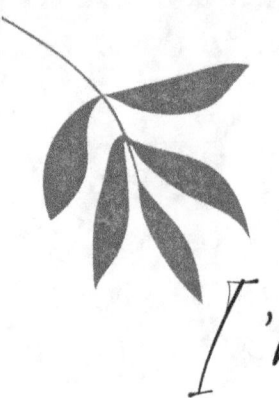

FIVE THINGS
I'm Grateful For

In a world full of chaos, ground yourself with
the beautiful things in your life.

FIVE THINGS
I'm Grateful For

In a world full of chaos, ground yourself with the beautiful things in your life.

FIVE THINGS
I'm Grateful For

In a world full of chaos, ground yourself with the beautiful things in your life.

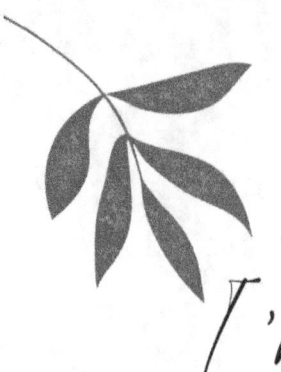

FIVE THINGS
I'm Grateful For

In a world full of chaos, ground yourself with the beautiful things in your life.

FIVE THINGS
I'm Grateful For

In a world full of chaos, ground yourself with
the beautiful things in your life.

FIVE THINGS
I'm Grateful For

In a world full of chaos, ground yourself with the beautiful things in your life.

FIVE THINGS
I'm Grateful For

In a world full of chaos, ground yourself with
the beautiful things in your life.

FIVE THINGS
I'm Grateful For

In a world full of chaos, ground yourself with
the beautiful things in your life.

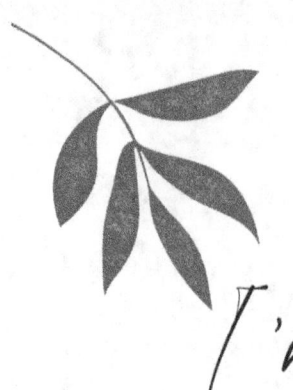

FIVE THINGS
I'm Grateful For

In a world full of chaos, ground yourself with the beautiful things in your life.

FIVE THINGS
I'm Grateful For

In a world full of chaos, ground yourself with
the beautiful things in your life.

FIVE THINGS
I'm Grateful For

In a world full of chaos, ground yourself with the beautiful things in your life.

1.

2.

3.

4.

5.

FIVE THINGS
I'm Grateful For

In a world full of chaos, ground yourself with
the beautiful things in your life.

FIVE THINGS
I'm Grateful For

In a world full of chaos, ground yourself with
the beautiful things in your life.

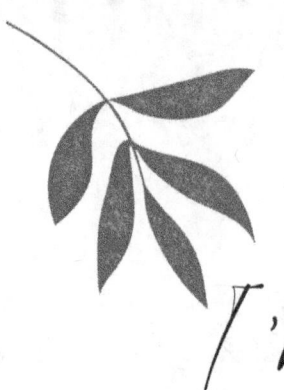

FIVE THINGS
I'm Grateful For

In a world full of chaos, ground yourself with the beautiful things in your life.

FIVE THINGS
I'm Grateful For

In a world full of chaos, ground yourself with the beautiful things in your life.

FIVE THINGS
I'm Grateful For

In a world full of chaos, ground yourself with the beautiful things in your life.

FIVE THINGS
I'm Grateful For

In a world full of chaos, ground yourself with the beautiful things in your life.

FIVE THINGS
I'm Grateful For

In a world full of chaos, ground yourself with
the beautiful things in your life.

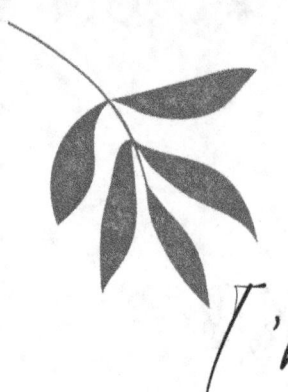

FIVE THINGS
I'm Grateful For

In a world full of chaos, ground yourself with the beautiful things in your life.

FIVE THINGS
I'm Grateful For

In a world full of chaos, ground yourself with
the beautiful things in your life.

FIVE THINGS
I'm Grateful For

In a world full of chaos, ground yourself with
the beautiful things in your life.

1.

2.

3.

4.

5.

FIVE THINGS
I'm Grateful For

In a world full of chaos, ground yourself with
the beautiful things in your life.

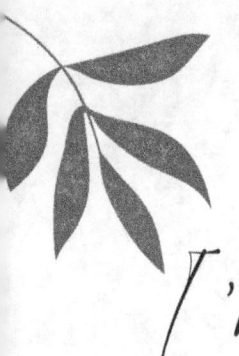

FIVE THINGS
I'm Grateful For

In a world full of chaos, ground yourself with the beautiful things in your life.

 1.

 2.

 3.

 4.

 5.

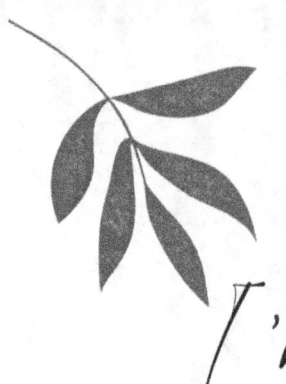

FIVE THINGS
I'm Grateful For

In a world full of chaos, ground yourself with
the beautiful things in your life.

FIVE THINGS
I'm Grateful For

In a world full of chaos, ground yourself with the beautiful things in your life.

FIVE THINGS
I'm Grateful For

In a world full of chaos, ground yourself with
the beautiful things in your life.

1.

2.

3.

4.

5.

FIVE THINGS
I'm Grateful For

In a world full of chaos, ground yourself with
the beautiful things in your life.

FIVE THINGS
I'm Grateful For

In a world full of chaos, ground yourself with the beautiful things in your life.

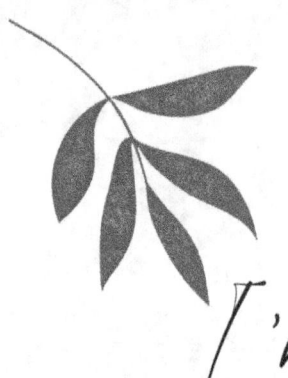

FIVE THINGS
I'm Grateful For

In a world full of chaos, ground yourself with
the beautiful things in your life.

FIVE THINGS
I'm Grateful For

In a world full of chaos, ground yourself with the beautiful things in your life.

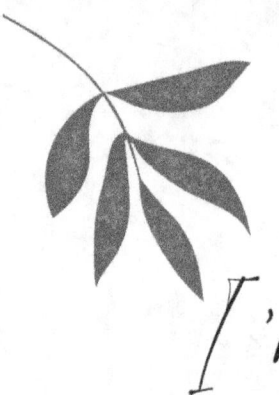

FIVE THINGS
I'm Grateful For

In a world full of chaos, ground yourself with the beautiful things in your life.

1.

2.

3.

4.

5.

FIVE THINGS
I'm Grateful For

In a world full of chaos, ground yourself with the beautiful things in your life.

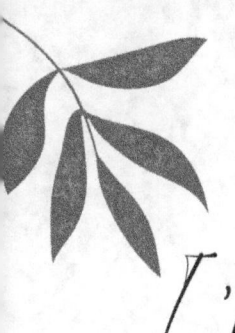

FIVE THINGS
I'm Grateful For

In a world full of chaos, ground yourself with the beautiful things in your life.

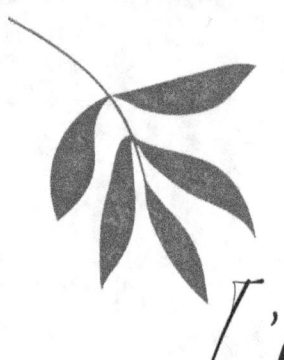

FIVE THINGS
I'm Grateful For

In a world full of chaos, ground yourself with the beautiful things in your life.

FIVE THINGS
I'm Grateful For

In a world full of chaos, ground yourself with the beautiful things in your life.

FIVE THINGS
I'm Grateful For

In a world full of chaos, ground yourself with
the beautiful things in your life.

FIVE THINGS
I'm Grateful For

In a world full of chaos, ground yourself with
the beautiful things in your life.

FIVE THINGS
I'm Grateful For

In a world full of chaos, ground yourself with
the beautiful things in your life.

FIVE THINGS
I'm Grateful For

In a world full of chaos, ground yourself with the beautiful things in your life.

FIVE THINGS
I'm Grateful For

In a world full of chaos, ground yourself with the beautiful things in your life.

FIVE THINGS
I'm Grateful For

In a world full of chaos, ground yourself with
the beautiful things in your life.

 1.

 2.

 3.

 4.

 5.

FIVE THINGS
I'm Grateful For

In a world full of chaos, ground yourself with
the beautiful things in your life.

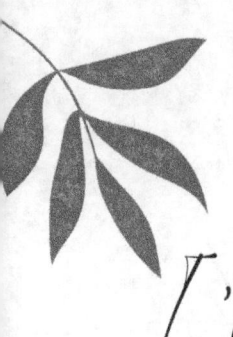

FIVE THINGS
I'm Grateful For

In a world full of chaos, ground yourself with
the beautiful things in your life.

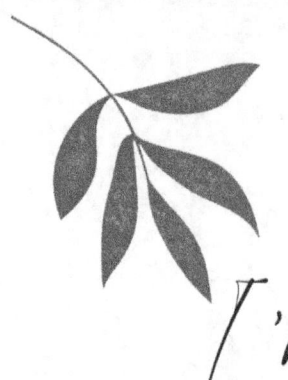

FIVE THINGS
I'm Grateful For

In a world full of chaos, ground yourself with the beautiful things in your life.

FIVE THINGS
I'm Grateful For

In a world full of chaos, ground yourself with
the beautiful things in your life.

FIVE THINGS
I'm Grateful For

In a world full of chaos, ground yourself with
the beautiful things in your life.

FIVE THINGS
I'm Grateful For

In a world full of chaos, ground yourself with
the beautiful things in your life.

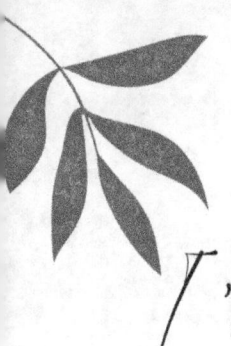

FIVE THINGS
I'm Grateful For

In a world full of chaos, ground yourself with
the beautiful things in your life.

FIVE THINGS
I'm Grateful For

In a world full of chaos, ground yourself with
the beautiful things in your life.

FIVE THINGS
I'm Grateful For

In a world full of chaos, ground yourself with
the beautiful things in your life.

FIVE THINGS
I'm Grateful For

In a world full of chaos, ground yourself with
the beautiful things in your life.

FIVE THINGS
I'm Grateful For

In a world full of chaos, ground yourself with
the beautiful things in your life.

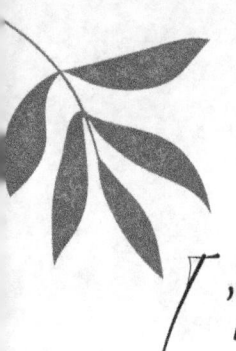

FIVE THINGS
I'm Grateful For

In a world full of chaos, ground yourself with the beautiful things in your life.

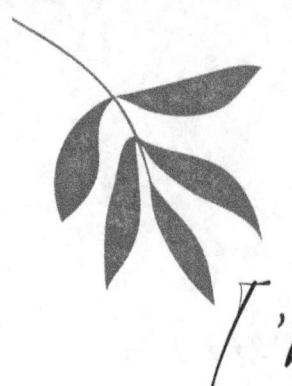

FIVE THINGS
I'm Grateful For

In a world full of chaos, ground yourself with the beautiful things in your life.

FIVE THINGS
I'm Grateful For

In a world full of chaos, ground yourself with the beautiful things in your life.

 1.

 2.

 3.

 4.

 5.

FIVE THINGS
I'm Grateful For

In a world full of chaos, ground yourself with the beautiful things in your life.

FIVE THINGS
I'm Grateful For

In a world full of chaos, ground yourself with
the beautiful things in your life.

FIVE THINGS
I'm Grateful For

In a world full of chaos, ground yourself with the beautiful things in your life.

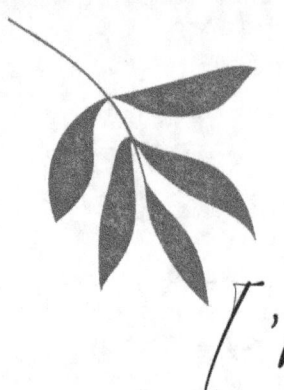

FIVE THINGS
I'm Grateful For

In a world full of chaos, ground yourself with the beautiful things in your life.

FIVE THINGS
I'm Grateful For

In a world full of chaos, ground yourself with
the beautiful things in your life.

FIVE THINGS
I'm Grateful For

In a world full of chaos, ground yourself with
the beautiful things in your life.

 1.

 2.

 3.

 4.

 5.

FIVE THINGS
I'm Grateful For

In a world full of chaos, ground yourself with the beautiful things in your life.

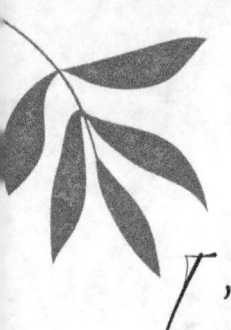

FIVE THINGS
I'm Grateful For

In a world full of chaos, ground yourself with the beautiful things in your life.

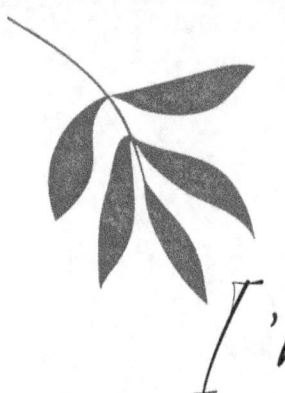

FIVE THINGS
I'm Grateful For

In a world full of chaos, ground yourself with the beautiful things in your life.

FIVE THINGS
I'm Grateful For

In a world full of chaos, ground yourself with the beautiful things in your life.

FIVE THINGS
I'm Grateful For

In a world full of chaos, ground yourself with the beautiful things in your life.

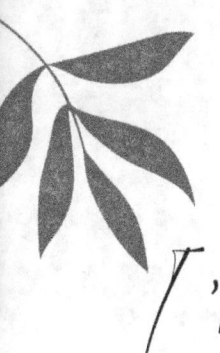

FIVE THINGS
I'm Grateful For

In a world full of chaos, ground yourself with the beautiful things in your life.

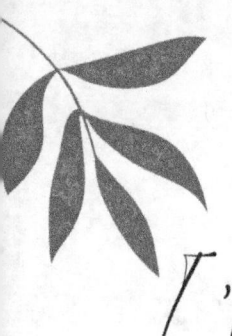

FIVE THINGS
I'm Grateful For

In a world full of chaos, ground yourself with
the beautiful things in your life.

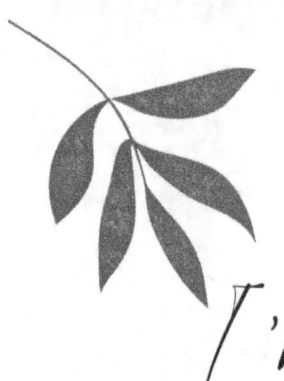

FIVE THINGS
I'm Grateful For

In a world full of chaos, ground yourself with
the beautiful things in your life.

FIVE THINGS
I'm Grateful For

In a world full of chaos, ground yourself with
the beautiful things in your life.

FIVE THINGS

I'm Grateful For

In a world full of chaos, ground yourself with
the beautiful things in your life.

1.

2.

3.

4.

5.

FIVE THINGS
I'm Grateful For

In a world full of chaos, ground yourself with the beautiful things in your life.

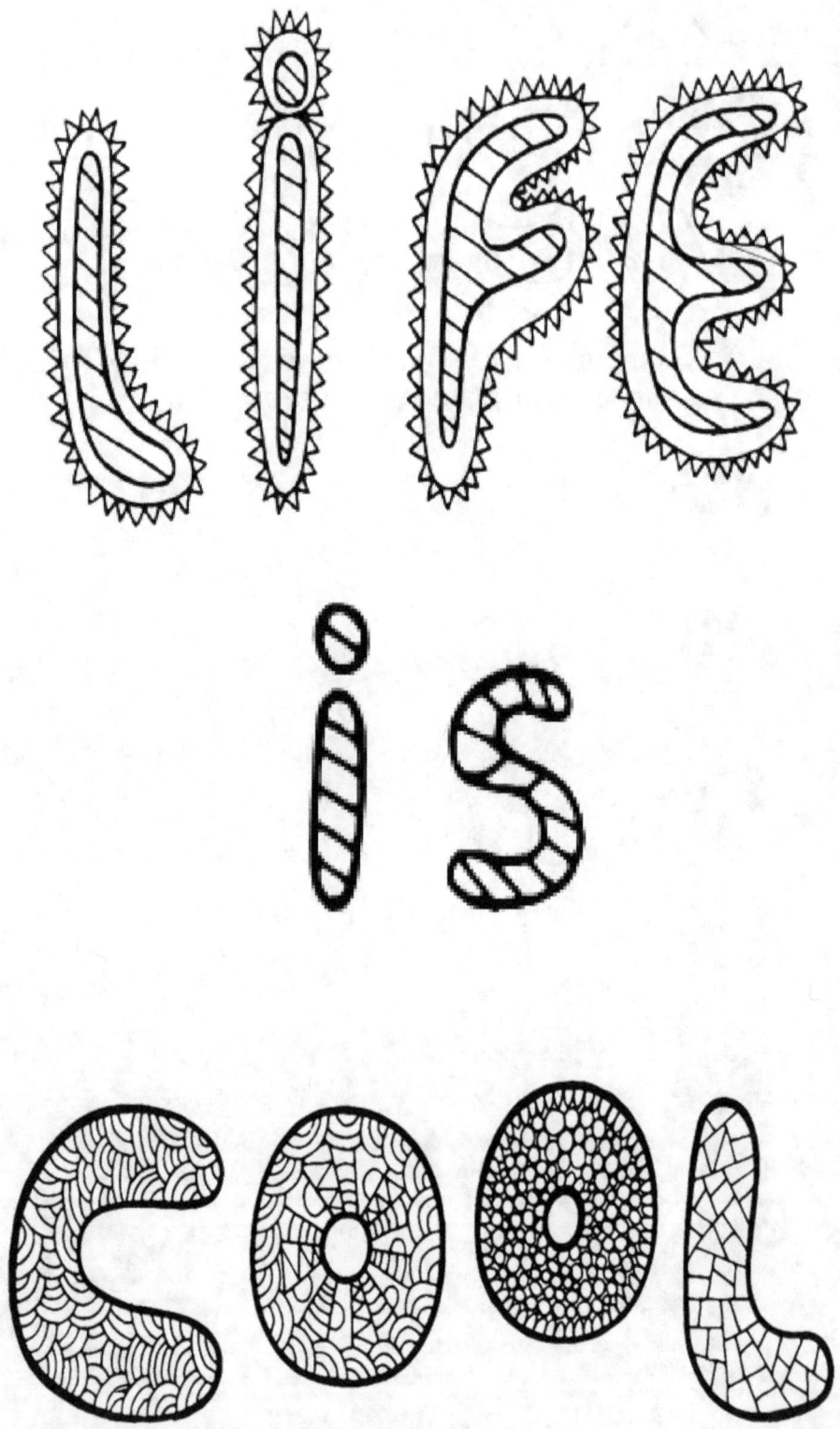

FIVE THINGS
I'm Grateful For

In a world full of chaos, ground yourself with
the beautiful things in your life.

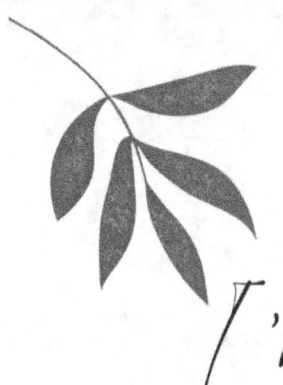

FIVE THINGS
I'm Grateful For

In a world full of chaos, ground yourself with the beautiful things in your life.

www.ingramcontent.com/pod-product-compliance
Lightning Source LLC
LaVergne TN
LVHW020422070526
838199LV00003B/248